This Journal Belongs to

Published by

Real Joy Publications

Printed in Great Britain
by Amazon

36189687R00066